To:

From:

Date:

Christian Art
GIFTS

© Christian Art Gifts, RSA
Christian Art Gifts Inc., IL, USA
Printed in China

"Be strong and courageous!
For the Lord your God is with you wherever you go."

Josh. 1:9

He made us, and we are His. We are His people, the sheep of His pasture.

Ps. 100:3

Give your burdens to the Lord, and He will take care of you.
Ps. 55:22

Let God transform you into a new person by changing the way you think.

Rom. 12:2

"God blesses those who work for peace,
for they will be called the children of God."

Matt. 5:9

"Anything is possible if a person believes."
MARK 9:23

I can do everything through Christ, who gives me strength.

Phil. 4:13

"Blessed are those who trust in the Lord and have made the Lord their hope and confidence."

Jer. 17:7

The Lord leads with unfailing love and faithfulness
all who keep His covenant and obey His demands.
Ps. 25:10

"Come to Me, all of you who are weary and carry heavy burdens, and I will give you rest."

Matt. 11:28

"Do not be afraid or discouraged,
for the Lord will personally go ahead of you."

Deut. 31:8

Those who live in the shelter of the Most High will find rest
in the shadow of the Almighty.

Ps. 91:1

"I will never fail you. I will never abandon you."
Heb. 13:5

Kind words are like honey – sweet to the soul and healthy for the body.
Prov. 16:24

"The joy of the Lord is your strength!"

Neh. 8:10

This is the day the Lord has made.
We will rejoice and be glad in it.
Ps. 118:24

Those who trust in the Lord will find new strength.
They will soar high on wings like eagles.
Isa. 40:31

"No eye has seen, no ear has heard, and no mind has imagined what God has prepared for those who love Him."

1 Cor. 2:9

I will rejoice in the Lord! I will be joyful in the God of my salvation!

Hab. 3:18

Nothing in all creation will ever be able to separate us from the love of God.

Rom. 8:39

My health may fail, and my spirit may grow weak, but God remains the strength of my heart; He is mine forever.

Ps. 73:26

See how very much our Father loves us, for He calls us
His children, and that is what we are!

1 John 3:1

"Blessed are all who hear the word of God
and put it into practice."
Luke 11:28

The Lord is my light and my salvation –
so why should I be afraid?

Ps. 27:1

"Be strong and courageous!
For the Lord your God is with you wherever you go."

Josh. 1:9

He made us, and we are His. We are His people, the sheep of His pasture.
Ps. 100:3

Give your burdens to the Lord, and He will take care of you.

Ps. 55:22

Let God transform you into a new person by changing the way you think.
Rom. 12:2

"God blesses those who work for peace,
for they will be called the children of God."

Matt. 5:9

"Anything is possible if a person believes."

Mark 9:23

I can do everything through Christ, who gives me strength.
Phil. 4:13

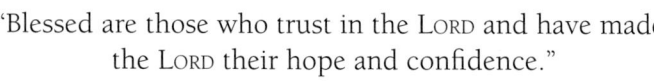

"Blessed are those who trust in the Lord and have made the Lord their hope and confidence."

Jer. 17:7

The LORD leads with unfailing love and faithfulness
all who keep His covenant and obey His demands.
Ps. 25:10

"Come to Me, all of you who are weary and carry heavy burdens, and I will give you rest."

Matt. 11:28

"Do not be afraid or discouraged,
for the Lord will personally go ahead of you."

Deut. 31:8

Those who live in the shelter of the Most High will find rest
in the shadow of the Almighty.

Ps. 91:1

"I will never fail you. I will never abandon you."
Heb. 13:5

Kind words are like honey – sweet to the soul and healthy for the body.

Prov. 16:24

"The joy of the Lord is your strength!"

Neh. 8:10

This is the day the LORD has made.
We will rejoice and be glad in it.
Ps. 118:24

Those who trust in the Lord will find new strength.
They will soar high on wings like eagles.

Isa. 40:31

"No eye has seen, no ear has heard, and no mind has imagined what God has prepared for those who love Him."

1 Cor. 2:9

I will rejoice in the LORD! I will be joyful in the God of my salvation!
Hab. 3:18

Nothing in all creation will ever be able to separate us from the love of God.
Rom. 8:39

My health may fail, and my spirit may grow weak, but God remains
the strength of my heart; He is mine forever.

Ps. 73:26

See how very much our Father loves us, for He calls us
His children, and that is what we are!

1 John 3:1

"Blessed are all who hear the word of God
and put it into practice."

Luke 11:28

The Lord is my light and my salvation –
so why should I be afraid?

Ps. 27:1

"Be strong and courageous!
For the Lord your God is with you wherever you go."

Josh. 1:9

He made us, and we are His. We are His people, the sheep of His pasture.

Ps. 100:3

Give your burdens to the Lord, and He will take care of you.
Ps. 55:22

Let God transform you into a new person by changing the way you think.
Rom. 12:2

"God blesses those who work for peace,
for they will be called the children of God."

Matt. 5:9

"Anything is possible if a person believes."

Mark 9:23

I can do everything through Christ, who gives me strength.
Phil. 4:13

"Blessed are those who trust in the Lord and have made the Lord their hope and confidence."

Jer. 17:7

The Lord leads with unfailing love and faithfulness
all who keep His covenant and obey His demands.

Ps. 25:10

"Come to Me, all of you who are weary and carry heavy burdens, and I will give you rest."

Matt. 11:28

"Do not be afraid or discouraged,
for the Lord will personally go ahead of you."

Deut. 31:8

Those who live in the shelter of the Most High will find rest in the shadow of the Almighty.

Ps. 91:1

"I will never fail you. I will never abandon you."

Heb. 13:5

Kind words are like honey – sweet to the soul and healthy for the body.

Prov. 16:24

"The joy of the Lord is your strength!"

Neh. 8:10

This is the day the LORD has made.
We will rejoice and be glad in it.
Ps. 118:24

Those who trust in the Lord will find new strength.
They will soar high on wings like eagles.

Isa. 40:31

"No eye has seen, no ear has heard, and no mind has imagined what God has prepared for those who love Him."

1 Cor. 2:9

I will rejoice in the LORD! I will be joyful in the God of my salvation!

HAB. 3:18

Nothing in all creation will ever be able to separate us from the love of God.

Rom. 8:39

My health may fail, and my spirit may grow weak, but God remains the strength of my heart; He is mine forever.

Ps. 73:26

See how very much our Father loves us, for He calls us
His children, and that is what we are!

1 John 3:1

"Blessed are all who hear the word of God
and put it into practice."
Luke 11:28

The LORD is my light and my salvation –
so why should I be afraid?

Ps. 27:1

"Be strong and courageous!
For the Lord your God is with you wherever you go."

Josh. 1:9

He made us, and we are His. We are His people, the sheep of His pasture.
Ps. 100:3

Give your burdens to the Lord, and He will take care of you.
Ps. 55:22

Let God transform you into a new person by changing the way you think.
Rom. 12:2

"God blesses those who work for peace,
for they will be called the children of God."

Matt. 5:9

"Anything is possible if a person believes."
Mark 9:23

I can do everything through Christ, who gives me strength.

Phil. 4:13

"Blessed are those who trust in the Lord and have made the Lord their hope and confidence."

Jer. 17:7

The Lord leads with unfailing love and faithfulness
all who keep His covenant and obey His demands.
Ps. 25:10

"Come to Me, all of you who are weary and carry heavy burdens, and I will give you rest."

Matt. 11:28

"Do not be afraid or discouraged,
for the Lord will personally go ahead of you."

Deut. 31:8

Those who live in the shelter of the Most High will find rest
in the shadow of the Almighty.

Ps. 91:1

"I will never fail you. I will never abandon you."

Heb. 13:5

Kind words are like honey – sweet to the soul and healthy for the body.

Prov. 16:24

"The joy of the Lord is your strength!"

Neh. 8:10

This is the day the Lord has made.
We will rejoice and be glad in it.

Ps. 118:24

Those who trust in the Lord will find new strength.
They will soar high on wings like eagles.
Isa. 40:31

"No eye has seen, no ear has heard, and no mind has imagined what God has prepared for those who love Him."

1 Cor. 2:9

I will rejoice in the Lord! I will be joyful in the God of my salvation!

Hab. 3:18

Nothing in all creation will ever be able to separate us from the love of God.

Rom. 8:39

My health may fail, and my spirit may grow weak, but God remains the strength of my heart; He is mine forever.

Ps. 73:26

See how very much our Father loves us, for He calls us
His children, and that is what we are!

1 John 3:1

"Blessed are all who hear the word of God
and put it into practice."

Luke 11:28

The LORD is my light and my salvation –
so why should I be afraid?

Ps. 27:1

"Be strong and courageous!
For the Lord your God is with you wherever you go."

Josh. 1:9

He made us, and we are His. We are His people, the sheep of His pasture.

Ps. 100:3

Give your burdens to the LORD, and He will take care of you.

Ps. 55:22

Let God transform you into a new person by changing the way you think.
Rom. 12:2

"God blesses those who work for peace,
for they will be called the children of God."

Matt. 5:9

"Anything is possible if a person believes."

Mark 9:23

I can do everything through Christ, who gives me strength.

Phil. 4:13

"Blessed are those who trust in the Lord and have made the Lord their hope and confidence."

Jer. 17:7

The LORD leads with unfailing love and faithfulness
all who keep His covenant and obey His demands.
Ps. 25:10

"Come to Me, all of you who are weary and carry heavy burdens, and I will give you rest."

Matt. 11:28

"Do not be afraid or discouraged,
for the Lord will personally go ahead of you."

Deut. 31:8

Those who live in the shelter of the Most High will find rest
in the shadow of the Almighty.

Ps. 91:1

"I will never fail you. I will never abandon you."

Heb. 13:5

Kind words are like honey – sweet to the soul and healthy for the body.
Prov. 16:24

"The joy of the Lord is your strength!"

Neh. 8:10

This is the day the LORD has made.
We will rejoice and be glad in it.
Ps. 118:24

Those who trust in the Lord will find new strength.
They will soar high on wings like eagles.

Isa. 40:31

"No eye has seen, no ear has heard, and no mind has imagined what God has prepared for those who love Him."

1 Cor. 2:9

I will rejoice in the Lord! I will be joyful in the God of my salvation!

Hab. 3:18

Nothing in all creation will ever be able to separate us from the love of God.
Rom. 8:39

My health may fail, and my spirit may grow weak, but God remains the strength of my heart; He is mine forever.

Ps. 73:26

See how very much our Father loves us, for He calls us
His children, and that is what we are!

1 John 3:1

"Blessed are all who hear the word of God
and put it into practice."

Luke 11:28

The Lord is my light and my salvation –
so why should I be afraid?

Ps. 27:1

"Be strong and courageous!
For the Lord your God is with you wherever you go."

Josh. 1:9

He made us, and we are His. We are His people, the sheep of His pasture.
Ps. 100:3

Give your burdens to the Lord, and He will take care of you.
Ps. 55:22

Let God transform you into a new person by changing the way you think.
Rom. 12:2

"God blesses those who work for peace,
for they will be called the children of God."

Matt. 5:9

"Anything is possible if a person believes."

Mark 9:23

I can do everything through Christ, who gives me strength.

Phil. 4:13

"Blessed are those who trust in the Lord and have made the Lord their hope and confidence."

Jer. 17:7

The LORD leads with unfailing love and faithfulness
all who keep His covenant and obey His demands.
Ps. 25:10

"Come to Me, all of you who are weary and carry heavy burdens, and I will give you rest."

Matt. 11:28

"Do not be afraid or discouraged,
for the Lord will personally go ahead of you."

Deut. 31:8

Those who live in the shelter of the Most High will find rest
in the shadow of the Almighty.

Ps. 91:1

"I will never fail you. I will never abandon you."
Heb. 13:5

Kind words are like honey – sweet to the soul and healthy for the body.

Prov. 16:24

"The joy of the Lord is your strength!"

Neh. 8:10

This is the day the LORD has made.
We will rejoice and be glad in it.
Ps. 118:24

Those who trust in the Lord will find new strength.
They will soar high on wings like eagles.

Isa. 40:31

"No eye has seen, no ear has heard, and no mind has imagined what God has prepared for those who love Him."

1 Cor. 2:9

I will rejoice in the Lord! I will be joyful in the God of my salvation!

Hab. 3:18

Nothing in all creation will ever be able to separate us from the love of God.
Rom. 8:39

My health may fail, and my spirit may grow weak, but God remains the strength of my heart; He is mine forever.

Ps. 73:26

See how very much our Father loves us, for He calls us
His children, and that is what we are!

1 John 3:1

"Blessed are all who hear the word of God
and put it into practice."

Luke 11:28

The Lord is my light and my salvation –
so why should I be afraid?

Ps. 27:1

"Be strong and courageous!
For the Lord your God is with you wherever you go."

Josh. 1:9

He made us, and we are His. We are His people, the sheep of His pasture.
Ps. 100:3

Give your burdens to the Lord, and He will take care of you.
Ps. 55:22

Let God transform you into a new person by changing the way you think.
Rom. 12:2

"God blesses those who work for peace,
for they will be called the children of God."

Matt. 5:9

"Anything is possible if a person believes."

Mark 9:23

I can do everything through Christ, who gives me strength.

Phil. 4:13

"Blessed are those who trust in the Lord and have made the Lord their hope and confidence."

Jer. 17:7

The LORD leads with unfailing love and faithfulness
all who keep His covenant and obey His demands.

Ps. 25:10

"Come to Me, all of you who are weary and carry heavy burdens, and I will give you rest."

Matt. 11:28

"Do not be afraid or discouraged,
for the Lord will personally go ahead of you."

Deut. 31:8

Those who live in the shelter of the Most High will find rest
in the shadow of the Almighty.

Ps. 91:1

"I will never fail you. I will never abandon you."

Heb. 13:5

Kind words are like honey – sweet to the soul and healthy for the body.

Prov. 16:24

"The joy of the Lord is your strength!"

Neh. 8:10

This is the day the LORD has made.
We will rejoice and be glad in it.
Ps. 118:24

Those who trust in the Lord will find new strength.
They will soar high on wings like eagles.
Isa. 40:31

"No eye has seen, no ear has heard, and no mind has imagined what God has prepared for those who love Him."

1 Cor. 2:9

I will rejoice in the LORD! I will be joyful in the God of my salvation!

HAB. 3:18

Nothing in all creation will ever be able to separate us from the love of God.
Rom. 8:39

My health may fail, and my spirit may grow weak, but God remains
the strength of my heart; He is mine forever.

Ps. 73:26

See how very much our Father loves us, for He calls us
His children, and that is what we are!

1 John 3:1

"Blessed are all who hear the word of God
and put it into practice."
Luke 11:28

The Lord is my light and my salvation –
so why should I be afraid?

Ps. 27:1

"Be strong and courageous!
For the Lord your God is with you wherever you go."

Josh. 1:9

He made us, and we are His. We are His people, the sheep of His pasture.
Ps. 100:3

Give your burdens to the Lord, and He will take care of you.

Ps. 55:22

Let God transform you into a new person by changing the way you think.
Rom. 12:2

"God blesses those who work for peace,
for they will be called the children of God."

Matt. 5:9

"Anything is possible if a person believes."

Mark 9:23

I can do everything through Christ, who gives me strength.

Phil. 4:13

"Blessed are those who trust in the Lord and have made the Lord their hope and confidence."

Jer. 17:7

The LORD leads with unfailing love and faithfulness
all who keep His covenant and obey His demands.
Ps. 25:10

"Come to Me, all of you who are weary and carry heavy burdens, and I will give you rest."

Matt. 11:28

"Do not be afraid or discouraged,
for the Lord will personally go ahead of you."

Deut. 31:8

Those who live in the shelter of the Most High will find rest
in the shadow of the Almighty.
Ps. 91:1

"I will never fail you. I will never abandon you."

Heb. 13:5

Kind words are like honey – sweet to the soul and healthy for the body.
Prov. 16:24

"The joy of the Lord is your strength!"

Neh. 8:10

This is the day the Lord has made.
We will rejoice and be glad in it.
Ps. 118:24

Those who trust in the LORD will find new strength.
They will soar high on wings like eagles.
Isa. 40:31

"No eye has seen, no ear has heard, and no mind has imagined what God has prepared for those who love Him."

1 Cor. 2:9

I will rejoice in the Lord! I will be joyful in the God of my salvation!

Hab. 3:18

Nothing in all creation will ever be able to separate us from the love of God.

Rom. 8:39

My health may fail, and my spirit may grow weak, but God remains the strength of my heart; He is mine forever.

Ps. 73:26

See how very much our Father loves us, for He calls us
His children, and that is what we are!

1 John 3:1

"Blessed are all who hear the word of God
and put it into practice."

Luke 11:28

The Lord is my light and my salvation –
so why should I be afraid?

Ps. 27:1

"Be strong and courageous!
For the Lord your God is with you wherever you go."

Josh. 1:9

He made us, and we are His. We are His people, the sheep of His pasture.
Ps. 100:3

Give your burdens to the Lord, and He will take care of you.

Ps. 55:22

Let God transform you into a new person by changing the way you think.
Rom. 12:2

"God blesses those who work for peace,
for they will be called the children of God."

Matt. 5:9

"Anything is possible if a person believes."
Mark 9:23

I can do everything through Christ, who gives me strength.

Phil. 4:13

"Blessed are those who trust in the Lord and have made the Lord their hope and confidence."

Jer. 17:7

The LORD leads with unfailing love and faithfulness
all who keep His covenant and obey His demands.
Ps. 25:10

"Come to Me, all of you who are weary and carry heavy burdens, and I will give you rest."

Matt. 11:28

"Do not be afraid or discouraged,
for the Lord will personally go ahead of you."

Deut. 31:8

Those who live in the shelter of the Most High will find rest
in the shadow of the Almighty.

Ps. 91:1

"I will never fail you. I will never abandon you."

Heb. 13:5

Kind words are like honey – sweet to the soul and healthy for the body.
Prov. 16:24

"The joy of the Lord is your strength!"

Neh. 8:10

This is the day the Lord has made.
We will rejoice and be glad in it.
Ps. 118:24

Those who trust in the Lord will find new strength.
They will soar high on wings like eagles.

Isa. 40:31

"No eye has seen, no ear has heard, and no mind has imagined what God has prepared for those who love Him."

1 Cor. 2:9

I will rejoice in the Lord! I will be joyful in the God of my salvation!

Hab. 3:18

Nothing in all creation will ever be able to separate us from the love of God.

Rom. 8:39

My health may fail, and my spirit may grow weak, but God remains the strength of my heart; He is mine forever.

Ps. 73:26

See how very much our Father loves us, for He calls us
His children, and that is what we are!

1 John 3:1

"Blessed are all who hear the word of God
and put it into practice."

Luke 11:28

The LORD is my light and my salvation –
so why should I be afraid?

Ps. 27:1

"Be strong and courageous!
For the Lord your God is with you wherever you go."

Josh. 1:9

He made us, and we are His. We are His people, the sheep of His pasture.

Ps. 100:3

Give your burdens to the Lord, and He will take care of you.
Ps. 55:22

Let God transform you into a new person by changing the way you think.

Rom. 12:2

"God blesses those who work for peace,
for they will be called the children of God."

Matt. 5:9

"Anything is possible if a person believes."

Mark 9:23

I can do everything through Christ, who gives me strength.

Phil. 4:13

"Blessed are those who trust in the Lord and have made the Lord their hope and confidence."

Jer. 17:7

The LORD leads with unfailing love and faithfulness
all who keep His covenant and obey His demands.

Ps. 25:10

"Come to Me, all of you who are weary and carry heavy burdens, and I will give you rest."

Matt. 11:28

"Do not be afraid or discouraged,
for the Lord will personally go ahead of you."

Deut. 31:8

Those who live in the shelter of the Most High will find rest
in the shadow of the Almighty.

Ps. 91:1

"I will never fail you. I will never abandon you."

Heb. 13:5

Kind words are like honey – sweet to the soul and healthy for the body.
Prov. 16:24

"The joy of the Lord is your strength!"

Neh. 8:10

This is the day the Lord has made.
We will rejoice and be glad in it.
Ps. 118:24

Those who trust in the Lord will find new strength.
They will soar high on wings like eagles.

Isa. 40:31

"No eye has seen, no ear has heard, and no mind has imagined what God has prepared for those who love Him."

1 Cor. 2:9

I will rejoice in the Lord! I will be joyful in the God of my salvation!

Hab. 3:18

Nothing in all creation will ever be able to separate us from the love of God.

Rom. 8:39

My health may fail, and my spirit may grow weak, but God remains the strength of my heart; He is mine forever.

Ps. 73:26

See how very much our Father loves us, for He calls us
His children, and that is what we are!

1 John 3:1

"Blessed are all who hear the word of God and put it into practice."

Luke 11:28

The Lord is my light and my salvation –
so why should I be afraid?

Ps. 27:1

"Be strong and courageous!
For the Lord your God is with you wherever you go."

Josh. 1:9

He made us, and we are His. We are His people, the sheep of His pasture.
Ps. 100:3

Give your burdens to the LORD, and He will take care of you.
Ps. 55:22

Let God transform you into a new person by changing the way you think.
Rom. 12:2

"God blesses those who work for peace,
for they will be called the children of God."

Matt. 5:9

"Anything is possible if a person believes."
Mark 9:23

I can do everything through Christ, who gives me strength.

Phil. 4:13

"Blessed are those who trust in the Lord and have made the Lord their hope and confidence."

Jer. 17:7

The LORD leads with unfailing love and faithfulness
all who keep His covenant and obey His demands.

Ps. 25:10

"Come to Me, all of you who are weary and carry heavy burdens, and I will give you rest."

Matt. 11:28

"Do not be afraid or discouraged,
for the Lord will personally go ahead of you."

Deut. 31:8

Those who live in the shelter of the Most High will find rest
in the shadow of the Almighty.

Ps. 91:1

"I will never fail you. I will never abandon you."

Heb. 13:5

Kind words are like honey – sweet to the soul and healthy for the body.

Prov. 16:24

"The joy of the Lord is your strength!"

Neh. 8:10

This is the day the Lord has made.
We will rejoice and be glad in it.
Ps. 118:24

Those who trust in the Lord will find new strength.
They will soar high on wings like eagles.

Isa. 40:31

"No eye has seen, no ear has heard, and no mind has imagined what God has prepared for those who love Him."

1 Cor. 2:9

I will rejoice in the LORD! I will be joyful in the God of my salvation!

Hab. 3:18

Nothing in all creation will ever be able to separate us from the love of God.
Rom. 8:39

My health may fail, and my spirit may grow weak, but God remains the strength of my heart; He is mine forever.

Ps. 73:26

See how very much our Father loves us, for He calls us
His children, and that is what we are!

1 John 3:1

"Blessed are all who hear the word of God and put it into practice."

LUKE 11:28

The Lord is my light and my salvation –
so why should I be afraid?

Ps. 27:1

"Be strong and courageous!
For the Lord your God is with you wherever you go."

Josh. 1:9

He made us, and we are His. We are His people, the sheep of His pasture.

Ps. 100:3

Give your burdens to the Lord, and He will take care of you.
Ps. 55:22

Let God transform you into a new person by changing the way you think.
Rom. 12:2

"God blesses those who work for peace,
for they will be called the children of God."

Matt. 5:9

"Anything is possible if a person believes."

Mark 9:23

I can do everything through Christ, who gives me strength.

Phil. 4:13

"Blessed are those who trust in the Lord and have made the Lord their hope and confidence."

Jer. 17:7

The Lord leads with unfailing love and faithfulness
all who keep His covenant and obey His demands.
Ps. 25:10

"Come to Me, all of you who are weary and carry heavy burdens, and I will give you rest."

Matt. 11:28

"Do not be afraid or discouraged,
for the Lord will personally go ahead of you."

Deut. 31:8

Those who live in the shelter of the Most High will find rest
in the shadow of the Almighty.

Ps. 91:1

"I will never fail you. I will never abandon you."

Heb. 13:5

Kind words are like honey – sweet to the soul and healthy for the body.
Prov. 16:24

"The joy of the Lord is your strength!"

Neh. 8:10

This is the day the Lord has made.
We will rejoice and be glad in it.
Ps. 118:24

Those who trust in the Lord will find new strength.
They will soar high on wings like eagles.
Isa. 40:31

"No eye has seen, no ear has heard, and no mind has imagined what God has prepared for those who love Him."

1 Cor. 2:9

I will rejoice in the Lord! I will be joyful in the God of my salvation!

Hab. 3:18

Nothing in all creation will ever be able to separate us from the love of God.
Rom. 8:39

My health may fail, and my spirit may grow weak, but God remains the strength of my heart; He is mine forever.

Ps. 73:26

See how very much our Father loves us, for He calls us
His children, and that is what we are!

1 John 3:1

"Blessed are all who hear the word of God
and put it into practice."
Luke 11:28

The Lord is my light and my salvation –
so why should I be afraid?

Ps. 27:1

"Be strong and courageous!
For the Lord your God is with you wherever you go."

Josh. 1:9

He made us, and we are His. We are His people, the sheep of His pasture.
Ps. 100:3

Give your burdens to the Lord, and He will take care of you.
Ps. 55:22

Let God transform you into a new person by changing the way you think.
Rom. 12:2

"God blesses those who work for peace,
for they will be called the children of God."

Matt. 5:9

"Anything is possible if a person believes."

Mark 9:23

I can do everything through Christ, who gives me strength.

Phil. 4:13

"Blessed are those who trust in the Lord and have made the Lord their hope and confidence."

Jer. 17:7

The LORD leads with unfailing love and faithfulness
all who keep His covenant and obey His demands.

Ps. 25:10

"Come to Me, all of you who are weary and carry heavy burdens, and I will give you rest."

Matt. 11:28

"Do not be afraid or discouraged,
for the Lord will personally go ahead of you."

Deut. 31:8

Those who live in the shelter of the Most High will find rest
in the shadow of the Almighty.

Ps. 91:1

"I will never fail you. I will never abandon you."

Heb. 13:5

Kind words are like honey – sweet to the soul and healthy for the body.
Prov. 16:24

"The joy of the Lord is your strength!"

Neh. 8:10

This is the day the Lord has made.
We will rejoice and be glad in it.

Ps. 118:24

Those who trust in the Lord will find new strength.
They will soar high on wings like eagles.
Isa. 40:31

"No eye has seen, no ear has heard, and no mind has imagined what God has prepared for those who love Him."

1 Cor. 2:9

I will rejoice in the Lord! I will be joyful in the God of my salvation!

Hab. 3:18

Nothing in all creation will ever be able to separate us from the love of God.

Rom. 8:39

My health may fail, and my spirit may grow weak, but God remains the strength of my heart; He is mine forever.

Ps. 73:26

See how very much our Father loves us, for He calls us
His children, and that is what we are!

1 John 3:1

"Blessed are all who hear the word of God
and put it into practice."
Luke 11:28

The Lord is my light and my salvation –
so why should I be afraid?

Ps. 27:1

"Be strong and courageous!
For the Lord your God is with you wherever you go."

Josh. 1:9

He made us, and we are His. We are His people, the sheep of His pasture.
Ps. 100:3

Give your burdens to the Lord, and He will take care of you.

Ps. 55:22

Let God transform you into a new person by changing the way you think.

Rom. 12:2

"God blesses those who work for peace,
for they will be called the children of God."

Matt. 5:9

"Anything is possible if a person believes."

Mark 9:23

I can do everything through Christ, who gives me strength.
Phil. 4:13

"Blessed are those who trust in the Lord and have made the Lord their hope and confidence."

Jer. 17:7

The LORD leads with unfailing love and faithfulness
all who keep His covenant and obey His demands.

Ps. 25:10

"Come to Me, all of you who are weary and carry heavy burdens, and I will give you rest."

Matt. 11:28

"Do not be afraid or discouraged,
for the Lord will personally go ahead of you."

Deut. 31:8

Those who live in the shelter of the Most High will find rest in the shadow of the Almighty.

Ps. 91:1

"I will never fail you. I will never abandon you."

Heb. 13:5

Kind words are like honey — sweet to the soul and healthy for the body.
Prov. 16:24

"The joy of the Lord is your strength!"

Neh. 8:10

This is the day the Lord has made.
We will rejoice and be glad in it.
Ps. 118:24

Those who trust in the LORD will find new strength.
They will soar high on wings like eagles.
Isa. 40:31

"No eye has seen, no ear has heard, and no mind has imagined what God has prepared for those who love Him."

1 Cor. 2:9

I will rejoice in the Lord! I will be joyful in the God of my salvation!
Hab. 3:18

Nothing in all creation will ever be able to separate us from the love of God.
Rom. 8:39

My health may fail, and my spirit may grow weak, but God remains
the strength of my heart; He is mine forever.

Ps. 73:26

See how very much our Father loves us, for He calls us
His children, and that is what we are!

1 John 3:1